Enjoying this Address Book?

Please leave a review because we would love to hear your feedback, opinions and advice to create better products and services for you!

Thank you for your support.
You are greatly appreciated!

BlankPublishers

This
Contact &
Address
Book
Belongs To

....

Name

Page#

Name

Page#

Name

Page#

Name

Address

Home   Mobile

Work

Email

Birthday

Name

Address

Home   Mobile

Work

Email

Birthday

Notes

Notes

Name

Address

Home   Mobile

Work

Email

Birthday

Name

Address

Home   Mobile

Work

Email

Birthday

Notes

Notes

. . . .

Name ____

Address ____

____

Home ______________ **Mobile** ______________

Work ____

Email ____

Birthday ____

. . . .

Name ____

Address ____

____

Home ______________ **Mobile** ______________

Work ____

Email ____

Birthday ____

. . . . Page#

Notes

Notes

Name

Address

Home   Mobile

Work

Email

Birthday

Name

Address

Home   Mobile

Work

Email

Birthday

Notes

Notes

Name

Address

Home   Mobile

Work

Email

Birthday

Name

Address

Home   Mobile

Work

Email

Birthday

Notes

Notes

Name

Address

Home   Mobile

Work

Email

Birthday

Name

Address

Home   Mobile

Work

Email

Birthday

Notes

Notes

Name

Address

Home   Mobile

Work

Email

Birthday

Name

Address

Home   Mobile

Work

Email

Birthday

Notes

Notes

Name

Address

Home   Mobile

Work

Email

Birthday

Name

Address

Home   Mobile

Work

Email

Birthday

Notes

Notes

Name

Address

Home   Mobile

Work

Email

Birthday

Name

Address

Home   Mobile

Work

Email

Birthday

Notes

Notes

Name

Address

Home   Mobile

Work

Email

Birthday

Name

Address

Home   Mobile

Work

Email

Birthday

Notes

Notes

Name

Address

Home   Mobile

Work

Email

Birthday

Name

Address

Home   Mobile

Work

Email

Birthday

Notes

Notes

Name

Address

Home   Mobile

Work

Email

Birthday

Name

Address

Home   Mobile

Work

Email

Birthday

Notes

Notes

Notes

Name

Address

Home   Mobile

Work

Email

Birthday

Name

Address

Home   Mobile

Work

Email

Birthday

Notes

Notes

Name

Address

Home   Mobile

Work

Email

Birthday

Name

Address

Home   Mobile

Work

Email

Birthday

Notes

Notes

Name

Address

Home   Mobile

Work

Email

Birthday

Name

Address

Home   Mobile

Work

Email

Birthday   Page#

Notes

Notes

. . . .

Name

Address

Home   Mobile

Work

Email

Birthday

. . . .

Name

Address

Home   Mobile

Work

Email

Birthday

. . . . Page#

Notes

Notes

Name

Address

Home   Mobile

Work

Email

Birthday

Name

Address

Home   Mobile

Work

Email

Birthday

Notes

Notes

Name

Address

Home   Mobile

Work

Email

Birthday

Name

Address

Home   Mobile

Work

Email

Birthday

Notes

Notes

Name

Address

Home   Mobile

Work

Email

Birthday

Name

Address

Home   Mobile

Work

Email

Birthday

Page#

Notes

Notes

Name

Address

Home   Mobile

Work

Email

Birthday

Name

Address

Home   Mobile

Work

Email

Birthday

Notes

Notes

Name

Address

Home   Mobile

Work

Email

Birthday

Name

Address

Home   Mobile

Work

Email

Birthday

Page#

Notes

Notes

Name

Address

Home   Mobile

Work

Email

Birthday

Name

Address

Home   Mobile

Work

Email

Birthday

Page#

Notes

Notes

· ·

Name

Address

Home   Mobile

Work

Email

Birthday

· ·

Name

Address

Home   Mobile

Work

Email

Birthday

· Page#

Notes

Notes

Name

Address

Home   Mobile

Work

Email

Birthday

Name

Address

Home   Mobile

Work

Email

Birthday

Page#

Notes

Notes

Name

Address

Home   Mobile

Work

Email

Birthday

Name

Address

Home   Mobile

Work

Email

Birthday

Notes

Notes

Name

Address

Home   Mobile

Work

Email

Birthday

Name

Address

Home   Mobile

Work

Email

Birthday

Notes

Notes

Name

Address

Home   Mobile

Work

Email

Birthday

Name

Address

Home   Mobile

Work

Email

Birthday

Notes

Notes

. . . . • • • • • • • • • • • • • • • • • • . . . .

Name
____

Address
____

____

Home _________________ Mobile _________________

Work _________________

Email _________________

Birthday _________________

. . . . • • • • • • • • • • • • • • • • • • . . . .

Name
____

Address
____

____

Home _________________ Mobile _________________

Work _________________

Email _________________

Birthday _________________

. . . . • • • • • • • • • • • • • • • • • . . . . Page#

Notes

Notes

Name

Address

Home   Mobile

Work

Email

Birthday

Name

Address

Home   Mobile

Work

Email

Birthday

Notes

Notes

Name

Address

Home   Mobile

Work

Email

Birthday

Name

Address

Home   Mobile

Work

Email

Birthday

Notes

Notes

Name

Address

Home   Mobile

Work

Email

Birthday

Name

Address

Home   Mobile

Work

Email

Birthday

Notes

Notes

Name

Address

Home   Mobile

Work

Email

Birthday

Name

Address

Home   Mobile

Work

Email

Birthday

Notes

Notes

Name

Address

Home   Mobile

Work

Email

Birthday

Name

Address

Home   Mobile

Work

Email

Birthday

Notes

Notes

Name

Address

Home   Mobile

Work

Email

Birthday

Name

Address

Home   Mobile

Work

Email

Birthday

Notes

Notes

Name

Address

Home   Mobile

Work

Email

Birthday

Name

Address

Home   Mobile

Work

Email

Birthday

Notes

Notes

Name

Address

Home   Mobile

Work

Email

Birthday

Name

Address

Home   Mobile

Work

Email

Birthday

Notes

Notes

· ·

Name ___________________________________

Address _________________________________

____

Home ____________ Mobile ____________

Work ___________________________________

Email ___________________________________

Birthday ________________________________

· ·

Name ___________________________________

Address _________________________________

____

Home ____________ Mobile ____________

Work ___________________________________

Email ___________________________________

Birthday ________________________________

· Page#

Notes

Notes

Name

Address

Home   Mobile

Work

Email

Birthday

Name

Address

Home   Mobile

Work

Email

Birthday

Notes

Notes

. . . .

Name

Address

Home   Mobile

Work

Email

Birthday

. . . .

Name

Address

Home   Mobile

Work

Email

Birthday

. . . . Page#

Notes

Notes

Name

Address

Home   Mobile

Work

Email

Birthday

Name

Address

Home   Mobile

Work

Email

Birthday

Notes

Notes

Name

Address

Home   Mobile

Work

Email

Birthday

Name

Address

Home   Mobile

Work

Email

Birthday

Notes

Notes

Name

Address

Home   Mobile

Work

Email

Birthday

Name

Address

Home   Mobile

Work

Email

Birthday

Notes

Notes

Name

Address

Home   Mobile

Work

Email

Birthday

Name

Address

Home   Mobile

Work

Email

Birthday

Page#

Notes

Notes

Name

Address

Home   Mobile

Work

Email

Birthday

Name

Address

Home   Mobile

Work

Email

Birthday

Page#

Notes

Notes

Name

Address

Home   Mobile

Work

Email

Birthday

Name

Address

Home   Mobile

Work

Email

Birthday

Notes

Notes

Name

Address

Home   Mobile

Work

Email

Birthday

Name

Address

Home   Mobile

Work

Email

Birthday

Notes

Notes

Name

Address

Home   Mobile

Work

Email

Birthday

Name

Address

Home   Mobile

Work

Email

Birthday

Page#

Notes

Notes

Name

Address

Home   Mobile

Work

Email

Birthday

Name

Address

Home   Mobile

Work

Email

Birthday

Notes

Notes

Name

Address

Home   Mobile

Work

Email

Birthday

Name

Address

Home   Mobile

Work

Email

Birthday

Notes

Notes

Name

Address

Home   Mobile

Work

Email

Birthday

Name

Address

Home   Mobile

Work

Email

Birthday

Page#

Notes

Notes

Name

Address

Home   Mobile

Work

Email

Birthday

Name

Address

Home   Mobile

Work

Email

Birthday

Notes

Notes

Name

Address

Home   Mobile

Work

Email

Birthday

Name

Address

Home   Mobile

Work

Email

Birthday

Page#

Notes

Notes

. . . .

Name

Address

Home   Mobile

Work

Email

Birthday

. . . .

Name

Address

Home   Mobile

Work

Email

Birthday

. . . . Page#

Notes

Notes

Name

Address

Home   Mobile

Work

Email

Birthday

Name

Address

Home   Mobile

Work

Email

Birthday

Notes

Notes

. . . .

Name ____

Address ____

____

Home ________________ Mobile ______________________

Work ____

Email ____

Birthday ____

. . . .

Name ____

Address ____

____

Home ________________ Mobile ______________________

Work ____

Email ____

Birthday ____

. . . . Page#

Notes

Notes

. . . .

Name

Address

Home   Mobile

Work

Email

Birthday

. . . .

Name

Address

Home   Mobile

Work

Email

Birthday

. . . . Page#

Notes

Notes

Name

Address

Home   Mobile

Work

Email

Birthday

Name

Address

Home   Mobile

Work

Email

Birthday

Notes

Notes

Name

Address

Home   Mobile

Work

Email

Birthday

Name

Address

Home   Mobile

Work

Email

Birthday

Notes

Notes

Name

Address

Home   Mobile

Work

Email

Birthday

Name

Address

Home   Mobile

Work

Email

Birthday

Notes

Notes

Name

Address

Home   Mobile

Work

Email

Birthday

Name

Address

Home   Mobile

Work

Email

Birthday

Page#

Notes

Notes

Name

Address

Home   Mobile

Work

Email

Birthday

Name

Address

Home   Mobile

Work

Email

Birthday

Notes

Notes

Name

Address

Home   Mobile

Work

Email

Birthday

Name

Address

Home   Mobile

Work

Email

Birthday

Notes

Notes

Name

Address

Home   Mobile

Work

Email

Birthday

Name

Address

Home   Mobile

Work

Email

Birthday

Notes

Notes

Name

Address

Home   Mobile

Work

Email

Birthday

Name

Address

Home   Mobile

Work

Email

Birthday

Notes

Notes

Name

Address

Home   Mobile

Work

Email

Birthday

Name

Address

Home   Mobile

Work

Email

Birthday

Notes

Notes

Name

Address

Home   Mobile

Work

Email

Birthday

Name

Address

Home   Mobile

Work

Email

Birthday

Page#

Notes

Notes

Name

Address

Home   Mobile

Work

Email

Birthday

Name

Address

Home   Mobile

Work

Email

Birthday

Notes

Notes

Name

Address

Home   Mobile

Work

Email

Birthday

Name

Address

Home   Mobile

Work

Email

Birthday

Notes

Notes

Name

Address

Home

Mobile

Work

Email

Birthday

Name

Address

Home

Mobile

Work

Email

Birthday

Notes

Notes

Name

Address

Home   Mobile

Work

Email

Birthday

Name

Address

Home   Mobile

Work

Email

Birthday

Notes

Notes

· ·

Name

Address

Home   Mobile

Work

Email

Birthday

· ·

Name

Address

Home   Mobile

Work

Email

Birthday

· Page#

Notes

Notes

Name

Address

Home   Mobile

Work

Email

Birthday

Name

Address

Home   Mobile

Work

Email

Birthday

Notes

Notes

Name

Address

Home   Mobile

Work

Email

Birthday

Name

Address

Home   Mobile

Work

Email

Birthday

Page#

Notes

Notes

www.ingramcontent.com/pod-product-compliance
Lightning Source LLC
Chambersburg PA
CBHW031228250726
48655CB00005B/1855